write the
TSC Service Information
For use with the Term Service Contract

An NEC document

April 2013

neccontract.com

NEC is a division of Thomas Telford Ltd, which is a wholly owned subsidiary of the Institution of Civil Engineers (ICE), the owner and developer of the NEC.

The NEC is a family of standard contracts, each of which has these characteristics:

- Its use stimulates good management of the relationship between the two parties to the contract and, hence, of the work included in the contract.

- It can be used in a wide variety of commercial situations, for a wide variety of types of work and in any location.

- It is a clear and simple document – using language and a structure which are straightforward and easily understood.

NEC3 how to write the TSC Service Information is one of the NEC family and is consistent with all other NEC3 documents.

ISBN (complete box set) 978 0 7277 5867 5
ISBN (this document) 978 0 7277 5925 2
ISBN (Term Service Contract) 978 0 7277 5891 0
ISBN (Term Service Contract Guidance Notes) 978 0 7277 5921 4
ISBN (Term Service Contract Flow Charts) 978 0 7277 5923 8
ISBN (how to use the TSC communication forms) 978 0 7277 5927 6

Reprinted 2016, 2017, 2019, 2020, 2021, 2022, 2024 (twice)

British Library Cataloguing in Publication Data for this publication is available from the British Library.

Typeset by Academic + Technical, Bristol

Printed and bound in Great Britain by Bell & Bain Limited, Glasgow, UK

CONTENTS

FOREWORD

I was delighted to be asked to write the Foreword for the NEC3 Contracts.

I have followed the outstanding rise and success of NEC contracts for a number of years now, in particular during my tenure as the 146th President of the Institution of Civil Engineers, 2010/11.

In my position as UK Government's Chief Construction Adviser, I am working with Government and industry to ensure Britain's construction sector is equipped with the knowledge, skills and best practice it needs in its transition to a low carbon economy. I am promoting innovation in the sector, including in particular the use of Building Information Modelling (BIM) in public sector construction procurement; and the synergy and fit with the collaborative nature of NEC contracts is obvious. The Government's construction strategy is a very significant investment and NEC contracts will play an important role in setting high standards of contract preparation, management and the desirable behaviour of our industry.

In the UK, we are faced with having to deliver a 15–20 per cent reduction in the cost to the public sector of construction during the lifetime of this Parliament. Shifting mind-set, attitude and behaviour into best practice NEC processes will go a considerable way to achieving this.

Of course, NEC contracts are used successfully around the world in both public and private sector projects; this trend seems set to continue at an increasing pace. NEC contracts are, according to my good friend and NEC's creator Dr Martin Barnes CBE, about better management of projects. This is quite achievable and I encourage you to understand NEC contracts to the best you can and exploit the potential this offers us all.

Peter Hansford

UK Government's Chief Construction Adviser
Cabinet Office

PREFACE

The NEC contracts are the only suite of standard contracts designed to facilitate and encourage good management of the projects on which they are used. The experience of using NEC contracts around the world is that they really make a difference. Previously, standard contracts were written mainly as legal documents best left in the desk drawer until costly and delaying problems had occurred and there were lengthy arguments about who was to blame.

The language of NEC contracts is clear and simple, and the procedures set out are all designed to stimulate good management. Foresighted collaboration between all the contributors to the project is the aim. The contracts set out how the interfaces between all the organisations involved will be managed – from the client through the designers and main contractors to all the many subcontractors and suppliers.

Versions of the NEC contract are specific to the work of professional service providers such as project managers and designers, to main contractors, to subcontractors and to suppliers. The wide range of situations covered by the contracts means that they do not need to be altered to suit any particular situation.

The NEC contracts are the first to deal specifically and effectively with management of the inevitable risks and uncertainties which are encountered to some extent on all projects. Management of the expected is easy, effective management of the unexpected draws fully on the collaborative approach inherent in the NEC contracts.

Most people working on projects using the NEC contracts for the first time are hugely impressed by the difference between the confrontational characteristics of traditional contracts and the teamwork engendered by the NEC. The NEC does not include specific provisions for dispute avoidance. They are not necessary. Collaborative management itself is designed to avoid disputes and it really works.

It is common for the final account for the work on a project to be settled at the time when the work is finished. The traditional long period of expensive professional work after completion to settle final payments just is not needed.

The NEC contracts are truly a massive change for the better for the industries in which they are used.

Dr Martin Barnes CBE

Originator of the NEC contracts

ACKNOWLEDGEMENTS

The original NEC was designed and drafted by Dr Martin Barnes then of Coopers and Lybrand with the assistance of Professor J. G. Perry then of the University of Birmingham, T.W. Weddell then of Travers Morgan Management, T.H. Nicholson, Consultant to the Institution of Civil Engineers, A Norman then of the University of Manchester Institute of Science and Technology and P.A. Baird then Corporate Contracts Consultant, Eskom, South Africa.

NEC wishes to acknowledge and thank the *how to write the TSC Service Information* project team for their input to this guidance.

The members of the Project team include:

    P. Higgins, BSc, CEng, FICE, FCIArb
    T. W. Weddell, BSc, CEng, DIC, FICE, FIStructE, ACIArb

Chapter 1 Introduction

The purpose of this guide is to help users to produce Service Information for the NEC3 Term Service Contract (TSC).

The convention of using italics for terms which are identified in the Contract Data of the TSC and capital initials for terms defined in the TSC has been used in this guide.

Good quality Service Information is vital to achieving better outcomes for service contracts and reducing misunderstandings and disputes. Service Information should be prepared with individual service requirements and the operation of the TSC in mind.

All NEC contracts refer to 'information' which sets out what the Parties are required to do under the contract. The obligation to work in accordance with that information is set out in the *conditions of contract*.

The diagram below shows the relationship between the constituent parts of a contract including the Service Information. Contract Data identifies the documents forming the contract. The *conditions of contract* refer to each part of the contract and require information to be stated in them. The form of agreement may be used to record the agreement between the Parties on the basis of the Contract Data, or the Parties may rely on an exchange of correspondence to establish the contract.

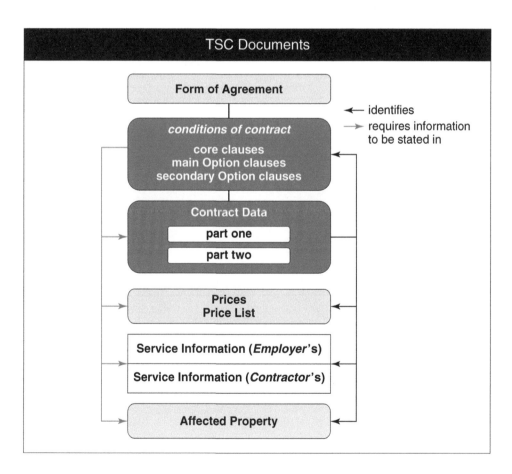

Information and documents required for the contract must be in the right part of the contract. If documents are located in the wrong place, it may cause confusion and risk that the documents are not properly incorporated. For example, information which describes the service must be identified in the Service Information. The diagram shows that Service Information is identified in Contract Data. Therefore, all documents and

information which describe the service or state constraints must be identified as Service Information and listed in Contract Data. This includes information contained within correspondence and minutes of meetings which describes the service to be provided.

The approach which results in the least uncertainty is to extract relevant information from correspondence and minutes of meetings and properly integrate it in the Service Information. Service Information will often consist of multiple documents and sections, in which case a contents list should be provided.

The clarity achieved by this contract structure and the separation of its parts is helpful to users and significantly reduces ambiguity and the potential for disputes. This guidance will help users to draft and assemble Service Information correctly. Chapter 2 describes the status of Service Information and the relationship between Service Information and the other parts of the TSC. Chapter 3 provides advice on drafting and how to achieve clarity. Chapter 4 is a checklist of information to be provided in Service Information, as required by the conditions of contract. Chapter 5 suggests an outline structure, including a list of topics to be considered for inclusion in the Service Information.

The requirement for good 'information' describing the work or services to be provided applies to all contracting systems. It is an objective of NEC to provide a contract which is clear and simple and promotes effective management and delivery of the *service*.

Chapter 2 The status of Service Information

The function of Service Information

Service Information is defined as

> **"11.2(15) Service Information is information which either**
>
> - **specifies and describes the *service* or**
> - **states any constraint on how the *Contractor* Provides the Service**
>
> **and is either**
>
> - **in the documents which the Contract Data states it is in or**
> - **in an instruction given in accordance with this contract."**

Service Information should be a complete and precise statement of the *Employer*'s requirements. If it is not, there is a risk that the *Contactor* will interpret it differently from the *Employer*'s intention.

Service Information prepared by the *Employer* is separated from Service Information prepared by the *Contractor* relating to his plan. The *Employer*'s Service Information is prepared first and the *Contractor* uses this to prepare the information relating to his plan. The *Employer*'s Service Information has priority over the *Contractor*'s Service Information under TSC clause 60.1(1).

If work is instructed through a Task Order, additional Service Information will be issued to the *Contractor* as part of the Order. Clause X19.2 states

> **"A Task Order includes**
>
> - **a detailed description of the work in the Task,**
> - **..."**

This information may add to the Service Information, or may simply identify the location of the work to be carried out, all other information being contained within the existing Service Information.

Service Information provided by the *Employer* includes

- technical information, specifications and drawings describing the *service,*
- constraints on how the *Contractor* Provides the Service, such as access requirements or specific safety requirements and
- *Employer*'s requirements for a plan to be prepared by the *Contractor*.

Service Information provided by the *Contractor* is particulars of the *Contractor*'s plan which he is required to prepare.

The *Contractor*'s primary obligation under TSC is stated in clause 20.1.

> **"20.1 The *Contractor* Provides the Service in accordance with the Service Information."**

When this clause is read in conjunction with clause 11.2(15) and the following clauses, the importance of Service Information is clear.

> **"11.2(4) A Defect is**
>
> - **a part of the *service* which is not provided in accordance with the Service Information or**
> - **a part of the *service* which is not in accordance with the applicable law or the Accepted Plan."**

> **"60.1 The following are compensation events.**
>
> **(1) The *Service Manager* gives an instruction changing the Service Information except**
>
> - **a change made in order to accept a Defect or**
> - **a change to the Service Information provided by the *Contractor* for his plan which is made either at his request or to comply with other Service Information provided by the *Employer*."**

The *conditions of contract* make frequent reference to Service Information as illustrated above and later in Chapter 4. Service Information is therefore central to the operation of the contract.

Service Information should be drafted in accordance with the three key objectives of NEC, namely flexibility, clarity and stimulus to good management.

The relationship between Service Information and Contract Data

Contract Data contains information needed to operate the contract, including the choice of main and secondary Options. Contract Data is the type of information often described in other forms of contract as the contract particulars or appendix. There are two parts. Part one contains the information provided by the *Employer* and part two is where the *Contractor*'s data and proposals are identified.

The TSC Guidance Notes contain detailed information on completion of the Contract Data.

The information set out in the Contract Data is not Service Information or Affected Property, but it identifies the documents which contain Service Information. The *Employer* identifies the documents which contain his Service Information in Contract Data part one. The *Contractor* identifies the documents which contain the Service Information for his plan in Contract Data part two. Where information is in non-documentary form, they should be identified and their availability and location stated.

Service Information should not contain information which repeats, contradicts or creates an ambiguity with any information contained within Contract Data or with the *conditions of contract*.

The following documents are identified within Contract Data and are not Service Information

- Partnering Information (if Option X12 is used),
- *service level table* (if Option X17 is used),
- Incentive Schedule (if Option X20 is used),
- matters to be included in the initial Risk Register,
- information describing the Affected Property and
- the plan (if required at tender stage).

A further distinction is that the *Service Manager* can instruct a change to Service Information but cannot change Contract Data once the contract is formed.

The relationship between Service Information and Affected Property

The *Contractor*'s obligations regarding Service Information and Affected Property are different; a clear separation between the two is required. Affected Property describes those areas where the *Contractor* carries out his activities. Normally these areas would comprise property belonging to the *Employer*. But they may be public areas such as highways where the *Contractor* may be required to carry out maintenance work such as street cleaning, gully emptying or refuse collection. Service Information describes what is to be done in these areas.

Affected Property is defined as follows:

> **"11.2(2) Affected Property is property of the *Employer* or Others which is affected by the work of the *Contractor* or used by the *Contractor* in Providing the Service and which is identified in the Contract Data."**

Affected Property is described in the Contract Data; this entry may include references to drawings and other documents, and, as with Service Information, is incorporated into the contract by reference to documents listed in Contract Data. The amount of detail included in the description of the Affected Property will depend on the *service*. There are several distinctions between Affected Property and Service Information. For example

- Affected Property cannot be changed by the *Service Manager* once the contract is formed. (Particular assets that are to be maintained within the Affected Property should be included within the Service Information as they may well need to change during the contract.)
- All ambiguities or inconsistencies in the description of the Affected Property and the related documents are dealt with under clause 17; this may result in a compensation event if a change to the Service Information is required (clause 60.1(1)).

Details of the Affected Property are provided to help the *Contractor* to prepare his tender, to decide his method of working and prepare the *Contractor*'s plan as required by clause 21.

Only factual information should be included.

The following example shows how Affected Property and Service Information can be separated.

Affected Property – Example Drawing List

Drawing No.	Description
0100	List of buildings to be maintained
0200	Property layout drawings
	Records of past maintenance
	Location of landscaping to be maintained

Service Information – Example Drawing List

Drawing No.	Description
0300	Replacement lift details
0400	Bulb/shrub planting locations

The relationship between Service Information and Price List

A clear distinction exists between Service Information and the Price List. Information in the Price List explains the Prices and should not describe the *service*. The *Contractor's* obligation is to Provide the Service in accordance with the Service Information. Statements about pricing of work should not be in the Service Information, as they neither specify or describe the *service* nor do they state constraints.

Information in the Price List does not change the obligation of the *Contractor* to Provide the Service in accordance with the Service Information.

Service Information as a contract document

Some forms of contract use provisions creating a hierarchy or priority of documentation as a means of resolving ambiguities and inconsistencies in or between documents. This is not the approach taken by NEC.

Priority clauses can interfere with the natural interpretation of documents as intended by the Parties. Such an indiscriminate approach to resolving ambiguities and inconsistencies can cause problems.

As explained in Chapter 1, the TSC describes the function of each document forming part of the contract. This provides clarity as to the relevance and purpose of each document in the contract. The *conditions of contract* then deal with any remaining ambiguity or inconsistency in or between the documents.

The TSC deals with ambiguities and inconsistencies between the documents forming the contract at clause 17.1.

> **"The *Service Manager* or the *Contractor* notifies the other as soon as either becomes aware of an ambiguity or inconsistency in or between the documents which are part of this contract. The *Service Manager* gives an instruction resolving the ambiguity or inconsistency."**

Such an instruction from the *Service Manager* changing the Service Information is a compensation event (clause 60.1(1), second bullet) except where the instruction is a

> **"change to the Service Information provided by the *Contractor* for his plan which is made either at his request or to comply with other Service Information provided by the *Employer*."**

There is no priority of documents in TSC other than the hierarchy of *Employer's* Service Information compared to *Contractor's* Service Information in clause 60.1(1). Service Information should be drafted to avoid any conflicts or contradictions. Service Information may consist of several documents drafted by different contributors. Ambiguities or inconsistencies between documents should be corrected before the documents are issued.

Chapter 3 Drafting Service Information

Incorporation of standard specifications

Service Information should be clear, complete and precise. Subjective terms should be avoided to reduce the risk of misinterpretation and dispute.

Standard specifications drafted for use on previous contracts or with other standard forms of contract should be reviewed and amended as appropriate, prior to incorporation.

Drafting shortcuts such as 'All references to Specification shall mean Service Information' are likely to cause problems. Each reference should be checked for correct use in relation to the duties and responsibilities of the *Employer, Contractor* and *Service Manager*.

The duties of the *Service Manager* are set out in the *conditions of contract.* The substitution of 'Service Manager' for 'Facilities Manager', for example as a drafting short-cut can cause confusion for the following reasons.

- The TSC *Service Manager* may not have the same duties as the Facilities Manager in other contracts. Some of the Facilities Manager's duties may be undertaken by the *Service Manager* and some by the *Adjudicator*.
- The TSC is more prescriptive on what can be done by the *Service Manager* on certification than other standard contracts.
- The 'acceptance' of a communication by a *Service Manager* may differ from an 'approval' given by a Facilities Manager in other contracts. TSC clause 14.1 states

  "The *Service Manager*'s acceptance of a communication from the *Contractor* or of his work does not change the *Contractor*'s responsibility to Provide the Service or his liability for his plan or his design."

Standard specifications should be checked to ensure consistency with other parts of the contract. For example, risk allocation varies from contract to contract and references to *Employer*'s and *Contractor*'s responsibilities within standard specifications need to be checked.

In their publication Managing Reality (Thomas Telford Publishing, 2012), Mitchell and Trebes give a number of examples of specification ambiguity when used with the NEC3 Engineering and Construction Contract. Their comments apply equally to the TSC.

Health and safety information

Clause 27.4 requires the *Contractor* to act in accordance with the health and safety requirements stated in the Service Information. Further comment on this clause is given in Chapters 4 and 5.

The *Employer* should consider how to deal with health and safety requirements and documentation carefully when preparing Service Information. The associated constraints on how the *Contractor* Provides the Service should be included in the *Employer*'s Service Information.

Many jurisdictions require health and safety risks to be evaluated by the *Employer* and then communicated to the *Contractor* as part of the procurement process. It may not be necessary to include the risk evaluation as a contract document, but it is necessary to check for consistency between the health and safety information and Service Information.

UK Specific illustration:

The Construction (Design and Management) Regulations 2007 require the preparation of Pre-Construction Information relating to health and safety and for this information to be provided to the *Contractor*. To the extent that a particular TSC includes construction activities, it is likely that provision of such information will be a requirement of the Regulations. This may contain information which is both Service Information and included under Affected Property. Care should be taken in deciding whether and how to include the Pre-Construction Information in the contract. Consider

- whether the information is included in the description of Affected Property (see Chapter 2),
- how changes and developments to the information will be administered
- which changes can only be made by an instruction of the *Service Manager* and which can be changed by the *Contractor* to suit his own proposals,
- the legal requirement for Pre-Construction Information to be issued to the *Contractor* and
- the time difference between formation of the contract and the *starting date* – during which the Pre-Construction Information may change.

In most cases, clarity will be achieved by keeping the Pre-Construction Information as a separate document. However, the Service Information must include information from the Pre-Construction Information which describes the *service* or states constraints, and the Affected Property entry must include or identify information which describes the areas where the *Contractor* will be working.

General drafting advice

The following description of NEC drafting style will help users draft Service Information and other contract documents clearly.

1. A basic objective of NEC contracts is that they should be clear and simple. The drafting delivers clarity and simplicity of language. Simplicity also follows from the design of the management processes in the contracts.

2. One of the objects of using simple language in the contracts is that they should be easy for people whose first language is not English to use. A further advantage is that the contracts can be translated into other languages accurately.

Vocabulary

3. Use the simplest possible words. Simple words have few syllables.

4. Do not use words which are not needed.

Sentences

5. Sentences should be as short as possible. Twenty words is fine. Never have more than forty. Use several short sentences instead of one sentence with several clauses.

6. Many statements are conditional. 'If this happens, the *Contractor* does this'. Put the condition first, not last and use 'if', not 'when'. 'If this happens, the *Contractor* does this.' [not: 'The *Contractor* does this when this happens.'] Use 'when' only if timing is implied as in clause 40.7.

7. Use commas properly. The pause which a comma creates can help understanding.

Bullets

8. Bullets are used when a clause includes a list. Do not use bullets for short lists with short descriptions. The following does not need to be bulleted:

    ''The *Contractor* arranges for 'Hail to the Chief' to be played by a brass band outside the *Service Manager*'s office at 9 a.m. on

    - Mondays,
    - Wednesdays,
    - Fridays and
    - his birthday.''

9. A useful check is that punctuation of bulleted sentences should work if the bullets are removed. Bullets end with a comma except the last but one which ends with 'and' or 'or' and the last which ends with a full stop. Do not put a comma before 'and'. 'And' replaces the comma before the last item on a list as above.

10. Whenever possible, put bullets at the end of a sentence. Having a bit more of the sentence after a bulleted list is clumsy as the reader does not expect the text and the sentence can become very long and not easy to understand.

11. Bullets are indented. Bullets within bullets should be avoided if possible. If used, as in clause 21.2, use a double indent.

Adjectives and Adverbs

12. Old-fashioned contracts use a lot of adjectives and adverbs. NEC contracts use the absolute minimum, which is hardly any. This is perhaps the most important drafting convention for NEC. Use an adverb or adjective only if it is really unavoidable.

13. Verbs and nouns are usually precise, adverbs and adjectives are usually imprecise. 'The *Contractor* does all urgent work quickly' is easy to understand. Unfortunately, you can argue about the meaning of 'urgent' (adjective) and 'quickly' (adverb). 'The *Contractor*' (noun), 'does' (verb) and 'work' (noun) are precise. To make the point absurdly, 'George ate a hefty meal unhurriedly' is vague but not meaningless. 'George ate a meal of 42 mouthfuls in 21 minutes' is boring but precise. Contracts are not intended to be a good read. They have to state who does what in words of unarguable precision and clarity.

14. Some adverbial phrases are as imprecise as adverbs, e.g. 'quickly' in 'come quickly' is obviously an adverb. So, in effect, is 'as soon as you can' in 'come as soon as you can'.

15. This text, for example, about extension of time, comes from clause 44(1) of the ICE conditions fifth edition, adverbs and adjectives in italics.

    '_____ or *exceptional adverse* weather conditions or other *special* circumstances of any kind _____ . be such as *fairly* to entitle the Contractor to an extension of time _____ Contractor shall within 28 days after the cause of the delay has arisen or as *soon thereafter* as is *reasonable* in all the circumstances deliver to the Engineer *full* and *detailed* particulars of any claim to extension of time _____ .'

16. It is impossible to decide whether an extension of time should be given and, if so, for how much, when and how described until the courts have decided what the adjectives and adverbs mean.

17. NEC drafting requires the absolute minimum of adverbs and adjectives. Some are innocuous as in clause 65.2 which uses the adjective 'wrong' as in 'wrong forecast'.

Clauses

18. Clauses should be as short as possible with no more than two sentences. They should cover only one subject.

Tenses

19. Use the present tense for all statements of what somebody must do or not do. It is seldom necessary to use another tense. 'If the sky has fallen down, the *Service Manager* decides what the *Contractor* will do' uses three tenses. 'If the sky falls down, the *Service Manager* decides what the *Contractor* does' uses only the present.

Capitals

20. Capital initials show that a term is defined in the contract. When drafting, test that a definition is right by putting it into the sentences where the defined term is used. These definitions are only abbreviations and must only be abbreviations. If there is anything to say about the defined term, it has to be in the clauses.

21. There are exceptions. *Service Manager*, *Employer* and *Contractor* have capitals but are not defined.

Particular words

22. 'May' in NEC means 'is allowed to' as in 'the *Service Manager* may give an instruction . . . .' Do not use it to mean that something might happen.

23. 'Any' can usually be deleted.

Multiple Alternatives

24. Either a, b, c or d. Bullet the alternatives if they are phrases of some length.

Chapter 4 TSC references to Service Information

The following table identifies where the *conditions of contract* refer to Service Information. Service Information should provide the information required by the contract and identify specific requirements for Providing the Service.

The references are in the order that they appear in the *conditions of contract* and cross referenced to the model form provided in Chapter 5.

TSC clause ref	Chapter 5	TSC clause description	Guidance on what should be in the Service Information
11.2(4)		A Defect is • a part of the *service* which is not provided in accordance with the **Service Information** or • a part of the *service* which is not in accordance with the applicable law or the Accepted Plan.	See Chapter 1.

11.2(6)	SI 1110
	SI 1200
		Disallowed Cost is cost which the *Service Manager* decides
		
		• is not justified by the *Contractor*'s accounts and records,
		• should not have been paid to a Subcontractor or supplier in accordance with his contract,
		• was incurred only because the *Contractor* did not
		  • follow an acceptance or
		  • procurement procedure stated in the **Service Information** or
		  • give an early warning which this contract required him to give
		
		and the cost of
		
		• Plant and Materials not used to Provide the Service (after allowing for reasonable wastage) unless resulting from a change to the Service Information,
		• resources not used to Provide the Service (after allowing for reasonable availability and utilisation) or not taken away when the *Service Manager* requested,
		• events for which this contract requires the *Contractor* to insure and
		• preparation for and conduct of an adjudication or proceedings of the *tribunal*
		
		and other amounts paid to the *Contractor* by insurers.
			State any acceptance or procurement procedures to be followed by the *Contractor*.

TSC clause ref	Chapter 5	TSC clause description	Guidance on what should be in the Service Information
11.2(7)		Equipment is items provided by the *Contractor* and used by him to Provide the Service and which the **Service Information** does not require him to include in the Affected Property.	
11.2(15)	SI 205	**Service Information** is information which either • specifies and describes the *service* or • states any constraints on how the *Contractor* Provides the Service and is either • in the documents which the Contract Data states it is in or • in an instruction given in accordance with this contract.	State any constraints on how the *Contractor* is to Provide the Service. See Chapter 1.
15.1	SI 205	The *Employer* provides the right of access for the *Contractor* to Affected Property as necessary for the work in this contract subject to any constraints stated in the **Service Information.**	State any constraints on access to the Affected Property eg. working hours.
15.2	SI 910	The *Employer* provides things which he is to provide as stated in the **Service Information.**	State those things which the *Employer* is to provide.
20.1		The *Contractor* Provides the Service in accordance with the **Service Information**.	See Chapter 1.

21.2	SI 400	The *Contractor* shows on each plan which he submits for acceptance
		
		• the *starting date* and the end of the *service period*,
		• the order and timing of the work of the *Employer* and Others as last agreed with them by the *Contractor* or, if not so agreed, as stated in the **Service Information,**
		• provisions for
		  • time risk allowances,
		  • health and safety requirements and
		  • the procedures set out in this contract,
		• the dates when, in order to Provide the Service in accordance with his plan, the *Contractor* will need
		  • access to the Affected Property as stated in the **Service Information,**
		  • acceptances,
		  • Plant and Materials, equipment and other things to be provided by the *Employer* and
		  • Information from Others,
			State any timing of the *Employer*'s activities which may affect the *Contractor*'s plan, see above. State when access to the Affected Property is to be provided. State any additional information that the *Contractor* is to show on the plan. This may include dates for submission of designs and samples, dates for information or actions by the *Employer* and *Service Manager* and the timing of any test or inspection.

TSC clause ref	Chapter 5	TSC clause description	Guidance on what should be in the Service Information
		• for each operation, a statement of how the *Contractor* plans to do the work identifying the principal Equipment and other resources which he plans to use and other information which the **Service Information** requires the *Contractor* to show on a plan submitted for acceptance.	
21.3		Within two weeks of the *Contractor* submitting a plan to him for acceptance, the *Service Manager* either accepts the plan or notifies the *Contractor* of his reasons for not accepting it. A reason for not accepting a plan is that • the *Contractor's* plans which it shows are not practicable, • it does not show the information which this contract requires, • it does not represent the *Contractor's* plans realistically or • it does not comply with the **Service Information.**	Refer to clause 21.2 above.
23.1	SI 305, 310	The *Contractor* submits particulars of the design of an item of Equipment to the *Service Manager* for acceptance if the *Service Manager* instructs him to. A reason for not accepting is that the design of the item will not allow the *Contractor* to Provide the Service in accordance with • the **Service Information,** • the Accepted Plan or • the applicable law.	State any design criteria for the design. State any procedures which the *Contractor* is to follow in carrying out his design and procedures for the submission of designs for acceptance by the *Service Manager* and Others.
25.1	SI 800	The *Contractor* co-operates with Others in obtaining and providing information which they need in connection with the *service*. He co-operates with Others and shares the Affected Property with them as stated in the **Service Information.**	Detail the activities of Others within the Affected Property.
25.2	SI 900	The *Employer* and the *Contractor* provide facilities and other things as stated in the **Service Information**. Any cost incurred by the *Employer* as a result of the *Contractor* not providing the facilities and other things which he is to provide is assessed by the *Service Manager* and paid by the *Contractor*.	State the facilities and other things that are to be provided by the *Employer* and *Contractor*.

TSC clause ref	Chapter 5	TSC clause description	Guidance on what should be in the Service Information
27.4	SI 1000	The *Contractor* acts in accordance with the health and safety requirements stated in the **Service Information**.	State any health and safety requirements for the contract which the *Contractor* must follow.
40.1	SI 605	The clauses in this clause only apply to tests and inspections required by the **Service Information** or the applicable law.	Detail the tests and inspections required, the results expected and which parties are involved in the test and inspection process.
40.2	SI 605	The *Contractor* and the *Employer* provide materials, facilities and samples for tests and inspections as stated in the **Service Information.**	State the materials, facilities and samples to be provided by the *Contractor* and the *Employer* for tests and inspections and the timing of these.
41.1	SI 605	The *Contractor* does not deliver those Plant and Materials which the **Service Information** states are to be tested or inspected before delivery until the *Service Manager* has notified the *Contractor* that they have passed the test or inspection.	State the Plant and Materials which are to be tested and inspected before delivery to the Affected Property, including details of tests or inspections.
50.4		In assessing the amount due, the *Service Manager* considers any application for payment the *Contractor* has submitted on or before the assessment date.	Identify any material which the *Contractor* is required to provide to assist the *Service Manager* in assessing the amount due.
51.1		The *Service Manager* certifies a payment within one week of each assessment date. The first payment is the amount due. Other payments are the change in the amount due since the last payment certificate. A payment is made by the *Contractor* to the *Employer* if the change reduces the amount due. Other payments are made by the *Employer* to the *Contractor*. Payments are in the *currency of this contract* unless otherwise stated in this contract.	Set out specific requirements for invoicing of the amount certified by the *Service Manager.*
60.1(5)		The *Employer* or Others do not work in accordance with the Accepted Plan or within the conditions stated in the **Service Information**.	Refer to clauses 25.1 and 25.2.

TSC clause ref	Chapter 5	TSC clause description	Guidance on what should be in the Service Information
60.1(11)		The *Employer* does not provide materials, facilities and samples for tests and inspections as stated in the **Service Information**.	Refer to clause 40.2.
70.2	SI 920	At the end of the *service period* the *Contractor* • returns to the *Employer*, equipment and surplus Plant and Materials provided by the *Employer*, • provides items of Equipment for the *Employer*'s use as stated in the **Service Information** and • provides information and other things as stated in the **Service Information**.	State the items of Equipment, information and other things which the *Contractor* is to provide for the *Employer*'s use at the end of the *service period*.
C and E 52.2	SI 1300	The *Contractor* keeps these records • accounts of payments of Defined Cost, • proof that the payments have been made, communications about and assessments of compensation events for Subcontractors and ther records as stated in the **Service Information**.	Detail any other records to be kept by the *Contractor*.
X4.1	SI 1400	If a parent company owns the *Contractor*, the *Contractor* gives to the *Employer* a guarantee by the parent company of the *Contractor*'s performance in the form set out in the **Service Information**. If the guarantee was not given by the Contract Date, it is given to the *Employer* within four weeks of the Contract Date.	Set out the form of parent company guarantee required.
X13.1	SI 1500	The *Contractor* gives the *Employer* a performance bond, provided by a bank or insurer which the *Service Manager* has accepted, for the amount stated in the Contract Data and in the form set out in the **Service Information**. A reason for not accepting the bank or insurer is that its commercial position is not strong enough to carry the bond. If the bond was not given by the Contract Date, it is given to the *Employer* within four weeks of the Contract Date.	Set out the form of performance bond required.
X19.1		(1) A Task is work within the *service* which the *Service Manager* may instruct the *Contractor* to carry out within a stated period of time.	Detail any additional procedures and forms to be used in the preparation of a Task Order.

TSC clause ref	Chapter 5	TSC clause description	Guidance on what should be in the Service Information

X19.6	SI 1700	The *Contractor* shows on each Task Order programme which he submits for acceptance
		
		• the Task starting date and the Task Completion Date,
		• planned Task Completion,
		• the order and timing of the operations which the *Contractor* plans to do in order to complete the Task,
		• provisions for
		  • float,
		  • time risk allowances,
		  • health and safety requirements and
		  • the procedures set out in this contract,
		• the dates when, in order to Provide the Service in accordance with the Task Order programme, the *Contractor* will need
		• access to the Affected Property,
		  • acceptances,
		  • Plant and Materials, equipment and other things to be provided by the *Employer* and
		  • information from Others, for each operation, a statement of how the *Contractor* plans to do the work identifying the principal Equipment and other resources which he plans to use and
		• other information which the **Service Information** requires the *Contractor* to show on a Task Order programme submitted for acceptance.
			State any additional information that the *Contractor* is to show on the programme. This may include dates for submission of designs and samples, dates for information or actions by the *Employer* and *Service Manager* and the timing of any test or inspection. Any requirements for the format of the programme should be stated, including the use of specific software and the requirement for hard or electronic copies. Any requirements for resource or financial data in the programme should also be stated.

X19.7		Within one week of the *Contractor* submitting a Task Order programme to him for acceptance, the *Service Manager* either accepts the programme or notifies the *Contractor* of his reasons for not accepting it. A reason for not accepting the Task Order programme is that • the *Contractor*'s plans which it shows are not practicable, • it does not show the information which this contract requires or • it does not comply with the **Service Information.**	Refer to clause X19.6 above.

Chapter 5 *Employer's* Service Information

There are many different ways to structure Service Information.

A straightforward Service Information structure is suggested in the NEC3 TSC Guidance Notes. This outline generally follows the sequence in which subjects arise within the conditions of contract. Many good Service Information documents have been compiled using this structure as a guide.

The example Service Information structure in this Chapter does not follow the order in which subjects appear in the *conditions of contract*. Instead it is an arrangement of topics for describing the *service*, flowing from general explanations and requirements to specific details. This structure also permits the voluminous documents (such as specifications) to be included as appendices to make navigation and digestion of other Service Information sections easier.

Guidance is provided for each Service Information section. This includes a checklist of topics to help users prepare a complete statement of the *Employer's* requirements. The checklist provides a list of topics which might need to be included – most contracts will not use all items.

Example Service Information structure

The numbering used below is indicative.

Section	Service Information (*Employer's*)
SI 100	Description of the *service*
SI 200	General constraints on how the *Contractor* Provides the Service
SI 300	*Contractor's* design
SI 400	The *Contractor's* plan
SI 500	Quality management
SI 600	Tests and inspections
SI 700	Management of the *service*
SI 800	Working with the *Employer* and Others
SI 900	Services and other things to be provided
SI 1000	Health and safety
SI 1100	Subcontracting
SI 1200	Acceptance or procurement procedure (Options C and E)
SI 1300	Accounts and records (Options C and E)
SI 1400	Parent company guarantee (Option X4)
SI 1500	Performance bond (Option X13)
SI 1600	Work call off arrangements
SI 1700	Task Order (Option X19)
SI 1800	*Employer's* service specifications and drawings

Guidance and checklist

This relates to the example Service Information structure shown above. Guidance relating to each Service Information section is provided in the grey boxes. A checklist of optional topics is also provided.

SI 100 Description of the *service*

> Provide a general description of the *service* to be carried out under the contract. Do not repeat the definition of the *service*.
>
> The general description should be consistent with the description in Contract Data part one, and identify the outline scope of the *service* to be provided. A general description of the *Contractor*'s plan may be included here. A detailed description is included in section SI 400.
>
> The *Employer*'s overall objectives for the *service* may also be stated, so that the *Contractor* understands them and can work with the *Employer* to achieve them.
>
> A description of services to be undertaken by the *Employer* or Others is in section SI 900.

Checklist	Explanation
SI 105 Description of the *service*	As above.
SI 110 Overall objectives	Explain 'why' the *service* is being undertaken. Specific objectives may include outcomes on safety, quality, time and functionality.

SI 200 General constraints on how the *Contractor* Provides the Service

> State any general constraints on how the *Contractor* Provides the Service, which are not covered by other Service Information sections.
>
> It can be useful to include the *service* objectives so that the *Contractor* can understand better the requirements of the Service Information. If they are included, state the requirements imposed on the *Contractor* in helping to achieve them.
>
> Constraints may include the checklist topics listed below. Constraints are restrictions on how the *Contractor* Provides the Service, not issues related to cash flow, funding or other requirements which conflict with the *conditions of contract*.

Checklist	Explanation
SI 205 General constraints	Examples of constraints. • Use of the Affected Property. • Access to the Affected Property. • Deliveries. • Noise and vibrations. • Working hours. • Parking. • Restrictions on the use of hazardous materials. • Storage of fuel and chemicals. • Pollution, ecological or environmental impacts. • *Employer* specific policies and procedures. • Constraints imposed to meet the requirements of Others.

SI 210 Confidentiality	Confidentiality and publicity restriction, and any acceptance procedures.
SI 215 Security and protection of the Affected property	Security requirements for the Affected Property and protection of the public.
SI 220 Security and identification of people	Security, vetting and identification of people working on or visiting the Affected Property. Requirements for people visiting the Affected Property.
SI 225 Protection of Affected Property	Specific requirements for the protection of Affected Property. Refer to details of Affected Property in Contract Data part one for location of existing things to be protected or procedures for identifying them. These details may include maps and drawings.
SI 230 Protection of the work on the Affected Property	Specific requirements for the protection of the work carried out by the Contractor against damage.
SI 235 Condition survey	Condition surveys to be carried out by the Contractor and any associated reinstatement works.
SI 245 Consideration of Others	Restrictions on work to avoid disturbance to the general public or occupiers of adjacent premises including Affected Property.
SI 250 Industrial relations	Specific requirements for the Contractor to comply with any industrial relations policies.
SI 255 Control of Contractor's personnel	Requirements for control of people working on the Affected Property. Permits and licences (for example permits to work).
SI 260 Cleanliness	Keeping the areas where the Contractor is working, clean and tidy.
SI 265 Waste materials	Removal of waste and restrictions on the disposal of waste material. Requirements for recycling.
SI 270 Deleterious and hazardous materials	Restrictions on the use of deleterious and hazardous materials.

SI 300 *Contractor*'s design

State the items of Equipment which the *Contractor* is to submit particulars of the design. The TSC is flexible in this respect, and allows the *Service Manager* to instruct submissions of additional items of Equipment during the contract, but the *Employer* should include here any items that he needs to review. State the criteria and procedures which the *Contractor* is to follow in carrying out his design, and procedures for the submission of design for acceptance by the *Service Manager*.

Checklist	Explanation
SI 305 Design submission procedures **TSC 23.1**	As above
SI 310 *Employer*'s requirements **TSC23.1**	Identify any *Employer*'s requirements for the design of Equipment

SI 400 *Contractor*'s plan

State any information additional to the requirements of TSC clause 21.2 that the *Contractor* is to include in the plan. This may include dates for submission of Equipment designs and samples, dates for information or actions by the *Employer* and *Service Manager*, and the timing of any test and inspection.

Any requirements for the format and content of the plan should be stated, including the use of specific software (if necessary) and the requirement for hard or electronic copies.

Checklist	Explanation
SI 405 Plan requirements **TSC 21.2**	As above.
SI 410 Methodology statement	Particular requirements for methodology statements, including any specific requirement for resource information.
SI 415 Work of the *Employer* and Others	The order and timing of the work of the *Employer* and Others to be included in the plan and information to be provided. Refer as necessary to sections SI 905 and SI 910.
SI 420 Information required	A schedule of information to be provided, who it is to be provided by, and the date by which it is to be provided.
SI 425 Revised plan	Any specific requirements for the submission of revised plans, such as an explanation of changes.

SI 500 Quality management

Detail the requirements for quality control and management.	
Checklist	**Explanation**
SI 505 Samples	State the materials and samples required including any procedures for submission and acceptance.
SI 510 Quality statement	Any requirement for a quality statement from the *Contractor*.
SI 515 Quality management system	Any requirements for a quality management system, including accreditations or legislative standards.

SI 600 Tests and inspection

Detail the tests and inspections required and which parties are involved in the test and inspection process. Tests and inspections may also be detailed within work specifications. Ensure consistency of drafting between this section and the contents of SI 1800.

Tests and inspections might be required for statutory compliance; in addition, state the requirements for

- Samples of Plant or Materials provided by the *Contractor*.
- Samples of workmanship.
- Plant and Materials.
- System tests.
- Computer software tests.
- Hygiene tests.
- Food quality checks.
- Performance tests.

State the materials, facilities and samples to be provided by the *Contractor* and the *Employer* for tests and inspections, and the timing of these.

State the Plant and Materials which are to be tested and inspected before delivery, including details of the test or inspection.

State any requirements for commissioning or performance tests in this section, in the same way that other tests and inspections are described.

Further guidance is in the NEC3 TSC Guidance Notes.

Checklist	Explanation
SI 605 Tests and inspections TSC 40.1 TSC 40.2 TSC 41.1 TSC 60.1(11)	Consider the following checklist for test and inspection details. • Objective, procedure and standards to be used. • When they are to be done. • Where they are to be done. • Who does the tests, and who is in attendance. • Testing and inspection method. • Access arrangements. • Information or instructions required to be provided. • Materials, facilities and samples to be provided. • Involvement of specialists. • Acceptable results and deviations. • Test environment. • Documents to be provided before and after the test. • Whether or not authorisation to proceed to the next stage of the work depends in the test results.

SI 610 Management of tests and inspections	Consider the requirement for a test and inspection schedule, containing all relevant information.
	State the procedures for submission and review.
SI 620 *Service Manager*'s procedures for inspections and watching tests	State any inspection procedures required by the *Service Manager*.

SI 700 Management of the *service*

The Contract Data identifies the *Employer, Service Manager* and *Contractor* and states what each is required to do. It is important, in using this section, not to contradict these obligations and duties. If any of their duties are delegated to Others, the extent of the delegation should be set out.

The TSC establishes a procedural framework based on good project management practice. It may be helpful to detail the communication procedures required to support this. This may include a framework of regular meetings, attendees required and outputs. Explain how people will be involved in the management of the service and how communications are to be managed.

Consider the use of a chart setting out the roles and responsibilities of the various parties involved.

State whether an internet based collaboration tool or other electronic communication system is to be used.

Identify any material to be provided to assist in assessing the amount due.

Describe the requirements for invoicing for payment.

Checklist	Explanation
SI 705 Management team – Others	As above.
SI 710 Communications	State any communication procedures which the *Contractor* is required to follow. Consider the following. • Meetings, attendees and meeting records. • Reporting requirements (e.g. progress reports). • Information requirements. • Electronic systems and communications. • Use of standard forms and templates. • Terminology and abbreviations.
SI 715 Payment provisions	• Material to be provided by the contractor by each assessment date to assist in assessing the amount due. • Requirements for invoicing of the certified amount.

SI 800 Working with the *Employer* and Others

Detail the activities of Others on the Affected Property.

The *Contractor* is required to co-operate with Others in obtaining and providing information which they need in connection with the service. State any requirements that have been agreed with Others.

Checklist	Explanation
SI 805 Sharing the Affected Property with the *Employer* and Others **TSC 25.1** **TSC 60.1(5)**	Provide a list of activities to be undertaken, explaining the following. • What is being done. • Who is doing it. • When it is being done, and for how long. • Where it is being done. • How the *Contractor* is to co-operate and share the Affected Property.
SI 810 Co-operation	Identify known information requirements, for the *Contractor* to obtain from Others or provide to Others, and timing.
SI 815 Co-ordination	State how the *Contractor* is to liaise with the *Employer* and Others for the co-ordination of work and access.
SI 820 Authorities and utilities providers	Identify works to be carried out by authorities and utilities providers. State the responsibility for enquiry, management, procurement, provision of notices and payment.

SI 900 Services and other things to be provided

State the services and other things that are to be provided by the *Employer* for use by the *Contractor*, and by the *Contractor* for use by the *Employer, Service Manager* or Others. Identify who they are provided for. It is not necessary to list things that the *Contractor* requires for his own use to Provide the Service.

State any requirements for quality and maintenance of services to be provided.

State those items of Equipment which the *Contractor* will be required to provide for the *Employer*'s use at the end of the *service period*.

State what information, including manuals, relating to the Equipment, Plant and Materials which the *Contractor* is to provide at the end of the *service period*.

Checklist	Explanation
SI 905 Services and other things for the use of the *Employer, Service Manager* or Others to be provided by the *Contractor* **TSC 25.2**	May include the following. • Accommodation. • Meeting rooms. • Storage facilities. • Catering. • Medical facilities and first aid. • Recreation. • Sanitation. • Security. • Copying. • Telephone, fax, radio or CCTV. • Computer equipment and services. • Sign boards and other signage. • Safety equipment and services. • Fences, screens and hoardings. • Postage. • Maintenance of access roads. • Temporary facilities. • Utilities, e.g. water and power. • Meter readings.
SI 910 Services and other things to be provided by the *Employer* **TSC 15.2, 25.2**	Same checklist as above. Consider the following also. • Access to the Affected Property. • Space for accommodation. • Plant and Materials.
SI 915 Access to information at the end of the *service period* **TSC 70.2**	State the *Employer*'s requirements for access to information at the end of the *service period* including timescale for the retention of information. Consider any need for computer software source code for example.
SI 920 Equipment provided to the *Employer* **TSC 70.2**	State any items of Equipment which the *Contractor* is to provide to the *Employer* at the end of the *service period*.

SI 1000 Health and safety

State any health and safety requirements which the *Contractor* must follow, in addition to the requirements of law. Refer to Chapter 4 for guidance on the inclusion of health and safety information in Service Information and Affected Property.

Checklist	Explanation
SI 1005 Health and safety requirements **TSC 27.4**	Details of any additional health and safety requirements, all which may include the following. • *Employer's* safety requirements. • Reporting requirements. • Safety management, supervision and qualifications. • Management of Subcontractors *l*. • Drug and alcohol policy. • Site induction procedures.
SI 1010 Method statements	Detail the operations for which the *Contractor* is required to submit method statements and risk assessments to the *Service Manager* for acceptance.
SI 1015 Legal requirements	If any health and safety duties are required by law, state who will perform them.
SI 1020 Inspections	State any requirement for review and inspection of *Contractor's* health and safety procedures by the *Service Manager*.

SI 1100 Subcontracting

The *Contractor* may subcontract work using an NEC contract. Any restrictions on the *Contractor* subcontracting work need to be set out.

The TSC does not provide for nomination of Subcontractors, for the reasons explained in the NEC3 Engineering and Construction Contract Guidance Notes. Alternatives to achieve similar objectives are

- make the *Contractor* responsible for all work; he may then subcontract parts and the *Service Manager* retains some control over the identity of the Subcontractors using TSC clause 26 or
- provide for separate contracts, with the *Service Manager* managing the time and physical interfaces between them.

Checklist	Explanation
SI 1105 Restrictions or requirements for subcontracting	State any restrictions and additional procedures which the *Contractor* must follow.
SI 1110 Acceptance procedures **TSC 26.3** **11.2(6)**	State any specific submission and acceptance procedures for proposed subcontracts not based upon an NEC contract. The basic requirement for submission and acceptance is dealt with at clause 26.3.

SI 1200 Acceptance or procurement procedure (Options C and E)

State any acceptance or procurement procedures which apply in addition to the constraints set out within section SI 1110. This is relevant to Options C and E where payment to the *Contractor* is based upon Defined Cost. The definition of Disallowed Cost refers to acceptance and procurement procedures stated in the Service Information.

SI 1300 Accounts and records (Options C and E)

Detail any records to be kept by the *Contractor*, in addition to those listed in clause 52.2.

Checklist	Explanation
SI 1305 Additional records **TSC 52.2 (Options C and E)**	List the additional records to be kept by the *Contractor*. This may include the following. • Timesheets and work allocations sheets. • Equipment records. • Records of stock holdings. • Forecasts of the total Defined Cost. • Specific procurement and cost reports. Define the format and presentation of records to be kept.

SI 1400 Parent company guarantee (Option X4)

Include the form of parent company guarantee required.

SI 1500 Performance bond (Option X13)

Include the form of performance bond required.

SI 1600 Work call off arrangements

If the work under the contract, or a part of it, is to be implemented on a "call off" basis following instruction of the *Service Manager*, include details of how the call off arrangement is to work.

SI 1700 Task Order (Option X19)

State any information additional to the requirements of TSC clause X19.6 that the *Contractor* is to include in the programme for a Task. This may include dates for submission of designs and samples, dates for information or actions by the *Employer* and *Service Manager*, and the timing of any test and inspection.

Any requirements for the format and content of the programme should be stated, including the use of specific software (if necessary) and the requirement for hard or electronic copies.

Checklist	Explanation
SI 1705 Programme requirements	As above.
SI 1710 Programme arrangement	Any specific arrangement of the programme, including any requirement for the programme to be produced in levels (summary level to detail level).
SI 1715 Methodology statement	Particular requirements for methodology statements, including any specific requirement for resource information.
SI 1720 Work of the *Employer* and Others	The order and timing of the work of the *Employer* and Others to be included in the programme and information to be provided. Refer as necessary to sections SI 905 and 910.
SI 1725 Information required	A schedule of information to be provided, who it is to be provided by, and the date by which it is to be provided.
SI 1730 Revised programme	Any specific requirements for the submission of revised programmes, such as an explanation of changes.

SI 1800 *Employer*'s service specifications and drawings

Include here the detailed service specifications and drawings which describe the *service*. A contents list may be provided or the documents themselves may be included or both. Guidance for including service specifications is in Chapter 3.

Checklist	Explanation
SI 1805 *Employer*'s service specification	Contents list or documents or both.
SI 1810 Drawings	Contents list or documents or both.

Chapter 6 Service Information provided by the *Contractor* for his plan

The purpose of this section of Service Information is to include the *Contractor*'s proposals and details for work which he is to plan. This may include Equipment, Plant and Materials, workmanship specifications, details and drawings. A contents list may be provided or the documents themselves may be included, or both.

Note that, where particulars of the *Contractor*'s plan are to be submitted for acceptance during the contract under clause 21.2, these submissions form part of the *Contractor*'s Service Information. In that case, this information will change over time.

Service Information prepared by the *Employer* is separated from any Service Information prepared by the *Contractor* relating to his plan. The *Contractor* cannot prepare his Service Information until the *Employer*'s Service Information has been prepared.

There should be no ambiguity or inconsistency between the *Contractor*'s Service Information and the *Employer*'s Service Information.

Care should be taken where the *Contractor* has offered an alternative proposal to the *Employer*'s Service Information. If the *Employer* decides to accept the alternative proposal, the *Employer*'s Service Information must be changed. There are two options for the *Employer* in this situation

- if the *Employer* assumes responsibility for the alternative proposal, then the *Employer*'s Service Information is changed to incorporate it. It is not included within the *Contractor*'s Service Information, or
- if the *Contractor* retains responsibility for the alternative proposal, then the *Employer*'s Service Information is changed to remove any redundant or conflicting content, and the alternative proposal is included in the *Contractor*'s Service Information.

Note that the *Employer*'s Service Information is treated as having priority over the *Contractor*'s Service Information under clause 60.1(1).